MORE THAN A CONQUEROR LLC

I0071813

So You Want To Write a Book

Sequoya Willis

So You Want To Write a Book

Publishers:
More Than A Conqueror LLC & Lulu
mymtaconline@gmail.com
http://mtaconline.webs.com
Printed in the United States of America
First Printing: November, 2012

ISBN: 978-1-300-44036-9

MORE THAN A CONQUEROR LLC

So You Want To Write a Book

Sequoya Willis

Dedication

This book is dedicated to my children T'Ajay Willis, Tajeona Brown, and Terrena Willis. May you live all of your hopes and dreams to the fullest. Mommy Loves you!

Step 1:

Selecting Your Title & Main Idea

Most people do not have a clue as to what their title will be. You are probably one of those people. I usually do not have my title ready. However, we need to keep our book organized while we are writing, otherwise the editing process will be gruesome and your readers will toss your book into the trash.

If you have a title available, that's great! If you do not, it's okay, too. The title of the book is the least of your worries. The important thing is to know what you want to write about. Most people already know the main idea of the book they are writing. If you do not have a main idea, yet, you should choose one now. The purpose of choosing a title or main idea, is so that we and our readers will know what we are writing about.

Below, is a sample title and a sample main idea that I will use for our sample book throughout this book. If I already chose my title, I would title my book, *"Birds of a feather."* If I am unable to think of a title at the time, I would simply select the main idea of the book, which would be, *"Birds and their groups."* Beneath my sample title and sample main idea, are blank lines for you to enter your title or main topic idea.

<u>Birds of a Feather</u>   <u>Birds and their groups</u>
   (Title)   or   **(Main Idea)**

Now enter your title or main topic idea in the available spaces below or on a separate sheet of paper, if you are planning to use this book again for another book project.

_____   _____
   (Title)   Or   **(Main Idea)**

Step 2:

Selecting Chapters & Topics

After you select your title or main idea, you will need to continue to keep your book as organized as possible during the writing process. Don't panic. I am going to teach you how.

It's time to select chapters for your book. It is difficult to create all of the chapters at one time for your book. If we waited to created chapters, we would never get the book done. Here is what you do. You will select your chapter titles later on. As you begin to write, the chapter titles will come to you. You may be sitting at the dinner table, riding the train, or taking a shower and a chapter title idea will pop into your brain. That is when you begin to create you chapter titles.

For now, we will create chapter topics. This will help us keep our writing organized in each section of the book. Later, as the titles for each chapter begins to comes to you, you will change the chapter topics into chapter titles.

In my sample book, *"Birds and their groups,"* I want to discuss certain things. The key is to ensure that you stay on topic. So, what we will do is create a chapter topic list. Check out my sample chapter topic list below.

Chapter Topic List

1. Wings
2. Feet
3. Types of birds
4. Feathers
5. Chirps
6. Eyes
7. Mental capacity

This means I plan on writing seven chapters in my book. I may get more chapter topic ideas and will add to the list, but for now, there will be only seven chapters. Your list may be longer and you may add to your list as you continue writing, as well.

Now, let's create you chapter topic list. If you already have a few chapter titles selected, you can write them down in place of a chapter topic. I gave you seven spaces, but you can write more as you create your list on a separate sheet of paper.

Chapter Topic List
1.
2.
3.
4.
5.
6.
7.

Great! You are on your way to becoming an author!

Step 3:

Selecting Your Sub-Topics

I know you are probably tired of organizing and ready to start writing your book. Patience, patience, patience. Everything I am telling you is crucial to your writing process. I wrote a book in 30 days for one of my clients and this is the process that helped me the most.

It's time to create a subtopic list. The subtopics will be listed within each chapter topic. This will help you stay organized within each of your chapter topics. You will automatically know what you are going to write about. Also, this will help you and/or your editor during the editing process.

Subtopics are the topics you want to write about within each chapter. Check out my sample subtopic list. I will list subtopics beneath one of my chapter topics. After, you look at my sample list, you will create your own.

A. **Wings**

- Color
- Length
- Width
- Birds

B. **Feet**

- Why are they webbed? (Explain)
- Are there different colors? (Explain)
- Do they have toes? (Explain)
- Do they have toe nails? (Explain)
- Do webbed feet make them walk differently?(Explain)

Here, I took two of my chapter topics and created subtopics beneath them. Notice, I wrote explain near some of them. That is because I am reminding myself that not only do I have to answer those questions, but I also have to give details about them. Each subtopic should take up at least 2-6 paragraphs. Remember, you are writing a book, so you want to give as much detail as possible. If you are writing a non-fiction book, you would follow the same process. You can use as many subtopics as you will need.

On a separate sheet of paper, create a list of subtopics using the diagram below.

_____

Chapter Topic
- _____ **(subtopic)**
- _____ **(subtopic)**
- _____ **(subtopic)**

_____

Chapter Topic
- _____ **(subtopic)**
- _____ **(subtopic)**
- _____ **(subtopic)**

Continue with this format until you have listed all subtopics for each chapter topic you created.

Step 4:

Formatting Your Page Layout

Formatting is very important. Especially, if you are going to self-publish. If your book is not formatted correctly, some of your pages will be coordinated the wrong way after printing. You have to be sure that your book is formatted the same size as the book size you are requesting. Also, the font style is important, because many printers do not have the same font style you have on your word processing software. They do how ever have basic styles that are used by most authors. Some of these styles include, Times New Roman, Arial, and Bookman Old Style (Most popular).

Font size is important, because you do not want your book's letters to be too big in your actual book. The size looks different to us on the computer screen, versus what it looks like in the actual book. I purposely made these words bigger than what an actual book would be, because I wanted the information to be clear and simple. I tailored it according to my reading audience.

We will also be learning how to format your margins, because you do not want to get your proof copy of your book and the words are scrunched up in the middle of the page and surrounded by large amounts of white space.

I know this sound like a lot of information, but it really isn't. I am going to make it clear and simple for you as we go along. Now let's begin.

Margins

I use Microsoft Word as my word processor, so the features are a bit different. However, you should be familiar with your word processor and will be able to find applications and tabs that we discuss. Any direction I give you here will be based on Microsoft Word's features, but try your best to find those same features on your word processor of choice.

Click on *"Page Layout"* on the top of your screen. Then click on *"Margins."* At the very bottom of the drop down menu, you will notice the words *"Custom Margins."* Click on *"Custom Margins."* Next to the word *"Top"* you are going to reset that margin to *0.5".* Next to the word *"bottom"* readjust that margin to *0.5".* Next to the word *"Left"* readjust that margin to *0.63".* Finally, next to the word *"Right"* readjust that margin to *0.5".*

Next, in that same tab, choose your orientation, which should be either *"portrait"* or *"landscape."* The picture shows you exactly how each one will look. Then, ensure that the section that reads, *"Multiple Pages"* reads as, *"Normal."* Finally, beside the words *"Apply To"* select *"Whole Document"* from the drop down menu and then click *"ok."* Your margins are now set.

Now let's adjust the size. Click on *"Page Layout"* on the top of your screen. Then click on *"Size."* The usual novel size is *"A5"* I usually choose *"A5"* for my books. However, you can choose any size you want for your books. Most work books are *"Letter Size."* You may want to look at some books in your house or look up book sizes on the internet and compare sizes to decide which book size is best for you. After, you decide on a size, click on it and you should notice your pages automatically resize. If it doesn't resize, it means you either chose *"Letter Size"* and the pages are already formatted to letter size. If not, it means you missed a step and should repeat the steps again.

So far so good right? We have formatted our margins and page size. Now let's format the font size and style.

Font Size and Font Style

Since this is your first book, we will use the usual font styles and sizes. When you write more books, you will be more familiar with size and style and can experiment a little. The traditional font size is 11. Most, book publishers request that you use this size, because it is easier to read. Go to the top of your page and on the tool bar, select font size 11.

There are three font styles that are compatible with the software applications used by most printers. They are *"Times New Roman"*

"Arial" and *"Bookman Old Style."* I prefer using *"Bookman Old Style,"* but you are welcome to choose any of the three. Go to the top of the page on your tool bar and select you font of choice. Font style drop down boxes are usually located next to font size drop down boxes.

Headers & Footers

If you take a look at the top of this page you will notice the book's title; *So You Want To Write a Book.* Next to it in the left hand corner would be my name *Sequoya Willis*. This is my header. Now if you scroll down to the bottom of the page, you will notice the publishing company's name and the page number. This is my footer.

You too, will need a header and footer to make your book look official. It is really simple. First, let me explain, you do not have to choose the same format for your headers and footers as I have. You may want you page numbers in you headers. You may not want to include the author's name. You may want your title in you footer. This is your baby. You place the information where ever you like. Just make sure it has an official look. I like to look at the layouts of books I read around the house and make my decision.

Now let's get started. On your tool bar at the top click on the *"Insert"* tab. Then select the arrow on the *"Header"* icon. Choose from the list of headers the style that best suits your style of book. If you are writing a children's book, you may only need to include page numbers in you header or footer.

After selecting your header style, you can delete the information the template has written by either clicking on the section or highlighting and deleting the information already there and then type in your own information.

After you are finished adding your header, click on *"Footer"* and choose your footer style. After choosing your footer style, you can delete the information the template has written by either clicking on the section or highlighting and deleting the information already there and then type in your own information. After you are done typing in your footer information click on *"Close Header & Footer."*

Font Sizes & Alignments

Usually for chapter pages, you would use center alignment and adjust your font sizes as you like. You should use a font size a little bigger than 11 for chapter titles. This helps the page stand out. However, to each his/her own.

You may also want to center your title page and dedication page. Again, to each his/her own. Now we get to the introductions, prologues, and body of the book. All of this should be in a justified alignment. Your words should be evenly aligned on both the left and right sides of the page; just as mine are here. Also take a look at my chapter pages and my copyright page. You may want to even copy mine. Feel free. Just be sure to change the information. You don't want me to take credit for your book.

Step 5:

Copyright & Order of Operation

Your copyright page is going to be left aligned. You can simply copy a copyright page from another book, but be sure to replace the author's information with your own. You can also Google a copyright page and copy and paste it to your own book and add or delete what you want and don't want. The copy right page is usually behind the very first page of your book. Before letting anyone view your book, or before attempting to self-publish, you should have already copy-written your book by visiting www.copright.gov. You can complete an online registration or mail the form in. I usually complete mine online because it is cheaper. It is currently $35.00. You wait a few weeks for your certificate to come in the mail. When copyrighting your book, you can send in more than one book at a time if you submit it under the same title of work. (Read more about copyrighting in my upcoming book *Copyright Anyone?*)

Order of Operation

Now it is time to fill your book up with a bunch of wonderful information. In the beginning you will need to insert title pages. You can do this by

1. Simply clicking on *"Insert"* and then click on *"Cover Page."* Enter all of the information you would like on your cover page.

2. Next click *"Insert"* on your tool bar and then click on *"Page Break"* and type or paste your copyright page.

3. Then click on *"Insert"* and then *"Cover Page"* and enter all of the same previous

information from the title page on the first page.

4. Then click *"Insert"* and *"Page Break"* and type up your dedication page.

5. Next, click *"Insert"* and type up your table of contents, which is optional. Not everyone has a table of contents.

6. Finally, click *"Insert"* and *"Page Break"* and then enter your first chapter page, which will either be *"Introduction," "Prologue," "Chapter one,"* or *"Your Chapter Title."*

7. Lastly, click on *"Insert"* and *"Page Break"* and then begin typing the contents of your first chapter.

When you are ready to insert a new chapter page, simply click on *"Insert"* and then click on *"Page Break."* Then type your chapter title on the blank page. After you type in your chapter title and adjust your fonts and alignments, click on "Insert" and then click on *"Page Break"* and begin typing the contents of your chapter, again. The reason we click on *"Page Break"* is because your book's formatting can be screwed up if you do not. Some printing machines only understand *"Page Break"* when another page is entered. Otherwise, you will have a bunch of blank spaces throughout your book. That doesn't mean that when you are typing and your words are spilling over you should hit *"Page Break."* Use *"Page Break"* only when you are inserting a chapter page.

Your pages should be in the following order. Of course, you can get creative and reorganize these pages. I am simply giving you a standardized format.

1. **Title Page**
2. **Cover Page**

3. **Title Page**

4. **Dedication**

5. **Table of Contents (Optional)**

6. **Intro, Prologue, or 1st Chapter Page**

7. **Chapter Contents**

8. **Next Chapter Page**

9. **Chapter Content**

Your last pages should be about the author and special thanks. Always be sure to include a page about your other products and services and how to contact you for events or book orders.

Editing

After you are done filling up your chapters, the editing process begins. You can hire an editor, have close friends, family members, or teachers edit your book for you, or you can take a chance and do it yourself.

If you would like quality service at an affordable rate that beats all other editors in the industry, contact More Than a Conqueror LLC at mymtaconline@gmail.com. You can look at the services provided for writers including writing packages for authors on the web at http://mtaconline.webs.com.

The next step in your process will be choosing a publisher. If you are interesting in self-publishing, you can check out my upcoming book So you want to Self-Publish, coming this Summer at http://mtaconline.webs.com or send an order request to mymtaconline@gmail.com. If you would like to self-publish but do not want the head-ache of doing it yourself, check out the special book publishing packages at http://mtaconline.webs.com.

Thank you for reading So You Want To Write A Book. I hope it was easy, clear, and concise.

About the Author

Sequoya Willis commands attention by captivating her audience with her real life stories and experiences. After being a victim of child abuse, she has transformed into a victorious voice for all who are or who were targets of child abuse and domestic violence. She touches the hearts, minds, and souls of various audiences from all walks of life. Her determination for victims to have victorious mind sets, healed hearts, and free spirits; motivates Sequoya to speak to individuals in prisons, religious groups, group homes, government and private agencies, schools, drug rehabilitation groups, parenting groups, women's groups, independent living groups, and many more. She delivers messages on *How to be Healed From Past Hurt and Pain, Stepping out of Abusive Mind Sets, Positive Thinking & Speaking, Reaching Goals and Bringing Dreams into Reality, How to Activate a Successful Mind Set,* and *Forgiveness*; too name a few.

Sequoya Willis is also an authoress who wrote and published inspiring memoirs about her own life; which brought awareness to child abuse and foster care in its full capacity. The memoirs are entitled *THE FIGHT OF MY LIFE: Memoirs of a Child Abuse Victim* and *THE FIGHT CONTINUES: Sagas of a Foster Child.* She is a community organizer and is most popular for creating Richmond's *FREE SHOPPING SPREE* for community residence who suffered from the country's recent recession during the Summer of 2009 with the help of project partners Alice Williams, Tonya Yard, and a not-for-profit organization called CAPUP. She wrote motivational and inspirational articles for the *Busy Bee Newsletter* in Broadwater Townhomes.

Currently, Ms. Willis is an internet talk show host for her own show called the Sequoya Show. The show provides inspirational and motivational encouragement to her audience. She is the CEO of More Than a Conqueror LLC. The business provides publishing, writing and speaking services to help people reach their goals, dreams, and business endeavors.

You can view interviews, videos, and more information about Sequoya Willis on her website http://fightofmylife.webs.com. To book her for speaking engagements, send emails to sequoyawillis@gmail.com. To find out more about Sequoya's business services please visit http://mtaconline.webs.com. To view episodes of her show visit http://sequoyashow.webs.com.

www.ingramcontent.com/pod-product-compliance
Lightning Source LLC
Chambersburg PA
CBHW070723210326
41520CB00016B/4429